Love, life and all that lies within

AF632821

Amy Alvarado

BookLeaf Publishing

Presentation by *BookLeaf Publishing*

Web: www.bookleafpub.com

E-mail: info@bookleafpub.com

ISBN: 9789357210324

First edition 2022

DEDICATION

For my kids

My Muse

She dances above the moon, in between sheets of dark magic
Just barely out of reach
She twirls in a cape of stars, but doesn't stay
Only sways to the music long enough to make me want more
She is my muse
And I watch her glow
She is my salvation
My heart
My true love
And she holds me in the way she dances
The way she moves
But she never stays
Only my heart does
I'm not meant to catch her
To keep her
To hold her
To breathe her in
Only to know she was there
Then she was gone
And I stay waiting…

What Do You See?

What do you see
When you look at me?
Small waist and small wrist
Or evil eyes and ready fists?
No one really wants to look behind the mask
Answers might just come too fast

Do I offend?
Because I never pretend
To make things pretty
When I know they are dirty
No one wants to acknowledge to beast
When it comes at night to feast

What must you think
When you hear my words?
Unabashed and uncensored, from mind to mouth
transferred?
No one wants to listen when the song isn't
sweet,
When the melodies don't drop the beat

Do you judge my skin,
Painted and tattooed with reminders of where
I've been?

Honey, I've got more stories than space to write
So they spill onto my body to tell my fight
No one wants to say I threaten their world
With all the truth Ive hurled

But...shhhh...take pause, take time
Remove the barriers
Find a way to unwind
Reach deep into your own existence
Appreciate my persistence
To live a truth without resistance
To conformity or society
A truth that is my own
And all that holds you back
Lies in what you won't face
Thinking life is some race
It's the journey that's true
Embrace it all, old and new
Scream out all the good and the rough
Are you brave enough?

Forgiveness

There is power in the forgiving
But sometimes there is even more power in the remembering
It's sticks on you
Settles onto the skin
Suffocating like a deep humidity
Burrowing into the bones

The forgiveness let's you breathe
But the remembering becomes a guard dog
Making a safe space for you
Building a wall
So you don't crawl
Back to the before times

And the remembering becomes survival
Reminds you of what you endured
Keeps your away
Covers you in a lead blanket
Safe, impenetrable

Forgiveness makes you human
Remembering makes you strong
I forgive today
I remember forever

Him

I took 2 steps
Toward him
He was pure sin
Holding a beer
Tight jeans
Smirk like the devil
Himself
Turn around
Walk another way
Any other way
But I always looked good
In black
And I'm ready to be ruined
I'm ready to drown
Bad never dresses in bad
It drips gold
And speaks honey
Tells you you're beautiful
Then pulls the rug
From under you
Laughs at your demise
I could pretend
Like I'm scared
Or angry
Or sad

But
I’m ready to be ruined
So instead
I’ll walk right up
And take his hand

Tears

I wake up fighting and I go to bed fighting
And I never see an end
I never get ahead
I never feel safe
Or peaceful
Or free

I fight every minute, every second of my life just
hoping to breathe
Just hoping to breathe
But I never can

There a tired that goes beyond tired
It seeps into your bones
And your mind
And your soul
It settles into you
And no amount of sleep takes it away
It is a tired that runs deep and wide
And over flows into everything that used to
bring you joy

Tears don't make it go away

You Should've Asked Me To Dance

You walked passed me
I pretended like I didn't see
But the crowded room meant your hand brushed mine
And the music swirled around us
And I knew you looked back
You should've asked me to dance

Maybe you felt too cool
Or not cool enough
While the drinks flowed free
And my eyes were so blurred I couldn't see
And the rhythm became a thing
That wrapped itself around me
You should've asked me to dance

When I wake up tomorrow and think of this night
And all the things that didn't go quite right
Only one will linger in shadows and light
Only one will be that missed, sad chance
And I'll sway to the beats I remember so well
The notes that took hold of me in fog that enveloped the whole crowd
You should've asked me to dance

It's Over

It took me forever
To breath you away
To remember that
You said I was yours
But never asked
If that's what I wanted

I thought it was so romantic
That we became "we"
Because that's how you
Made me forget "me"

And I still feel you when
Those songs come on
And I still can't skip over them
I sit in my silence

There are stains I still can't wash off
Stains I still scrub raw
Stains I miss when they are finally gone

And I hate myself in that moment
Because it's supposed to be so easy
Walk away
Slam the door

Don’t look back
Don’t answer

No one tells you that
Your mind and your heart are at war
And that too many times your heart wins
No one tells you that you stop
Looking in mirrors
Because your reflection makes you cringe

The Day I Drowned

What do I deserve?
Standing in the shadow of a crumbled foundation
Trying to pick up my pride
Dust off my heart
Reeling from the illusion that I built one day, one moment, years ago

I didn't care enough
Or did I care too much?
Too much to lift the veil that kept me dark, kept my eyes covered in a sheath of artificial happiness

And I wrote stories
Stories until the lead broke into pieces and the ink dried up
And I read them back to myself, fantasies of a land that never existed but in my own mind

What do I deserve?
Still sitting in the grief of a memory
The purpose muddled in the past of a different time, a different place, a different me

The present so bright the pain becomes
highlighted in the mundane

Should I have known?
But the human part, the vulnerable part never
wants to know
Instead, weaving strings of magical light,
making the world seem right
And I lived there, planted my feet on unstable
ground, didn't notice the tide coming in, higher
and higher
Oblivious until the day I drowned

Everything

I can only stand in your shadow sometimes and
look up in wonder
Everything about you is beautiful
I ride the coattails of your wings to be a part of
your SOAR
Everything about you is beautiful
Your tears, your scars, your invisible war
Your smile, your laugh, the lines in the corners
of your eyes
Your terror, your shame, your spirit, hidden and
booming at the same time
When a moment like this, fleeting and
insignificant, finds me lost and wanting…
Step back, step down, stillness for eternity
And you, always you
Raising my head, holding my heart…
Everything about you is beautiful.

I Write

I write because I feel
I feel so deeply and intensely
To my core
Through my soul
But most don't see
Because I've curated a mask
A mask that is hard
Bulletproof
So I write...

I write to remember
And to wallow
And to find my feelings
But most won't see
Because I hide
Behind walls
And under weighted blankets
So I write...

But I know we are connected
And we share moments
And pains
And experiences
So I write...
Will you read?

For Me

Woke up today and forgot
That where I am is where you're not
I check the closet one more time
But all that's there is mine
Standing all alone on this balcony
With only my agony
It wasn't over for me

It wasn't over for me
Why would you want to be free?
What was it I couldn't see?
What was it I couldn't be?
Because it wasn't over for me

Dark nights, awake until dawn
Still denying that you're gone
I look for signs but find none
Just reminders that we're done
I just don't want to believe
Because it's isn't over for me

My heart doesn't want to let go
My mind doesn't want to know
I watched you walk away, I watched you leave
But it was never over for me

Pain

I am wasting away
Rice paper thin
Brittle life
A playing card tower
Don't dare take a breath

I pray to my body
I pray for it to work
It never listens
I think it laughs
But my prayers continue
Soft, shadowy

I know I smiled before
And meant it
Crinkle wrinkles in the corners
Of my almond eyes
It's lost to me now

I pray outside of myself
For any part of me to work
Even for a short time
So I can catch the smile again
Make it real again

I rub my hands over my skin
I say to myself
"I've been good to you, haven't I?"
Haven't I?
There's never an answer
No instructions
If follow them to a tee

Instead I scratch out recipes
And hope they come out okay

Different Mind of Cowboy

I'm a different kind of country
Yeah, I drive down those country roads in my beat up truck
But on My cruise I see my brothers and sisters
Bent back
Sweaty brow
Carving out an existence
In fields that provide for everyone else

Hell, I'm country
But I'm a different kind of country
My bbq grill doesn't sizzle with a burger
But with the food de mis antepasados
The seasoned carne asada that makes the base of my beloved tacos
And my corn needs a lot more than a pat of butter

I'm down home country
Canal fishing country
But I'm a different kind of country
The backyard party doesn't start with Strait or Brooks

But with Selena and Celia and ends with Vicente
while my arms hang over the shoulders of my
cousins, drunk with love for la musica

And any place is a dance floor
Where we twirl to the cumbias
That have been listened to so many years before

I'm proud of my kind of country
A deep rooted, solid country
Where there is no "Hey, y'all"
But "que onda" y "simón"

I will always be country
My country
This is my history
This is my tribe
This is mi gente

Useless

This feeling so useless creeps up on me if I let it
Slow steps
Soft behind me
It hides when I turn around but I can feel it there

This feeling of useless can wrap itself around me
if I let it
Sticking on my skin
Light humming in my ear
In tbe middle of the night
When I can't sleep

But today I will do one thing
One baby step,
One thing
And I am strong

But today I will do finish one thing
Something small
One thing
And I am able

Ghosts and Demons

And the ghosts won't talk to me
And the demons don't even see
I'm falling into a big black whole
Forget what ever you heard about a soul

And when the Sun goes down
And I'm swallowed by the ground
I won't call your name
To help with what remains

When the world stops spinning
And I think I might be winning
Then it all falls apart
And I'm back at the start
Don't come for me

When I'm balancing on a beam
That is way thinner then it seems
And my legs begin to shake
All I ever knew is at stake
Don't come for me

Broken can be fixed
Even when held together with sticks
And glue and a quiet prayer

While i wait and lay here
Knowing a crack or scratch
Or pieces that don't match
Are okay when I've been the one
Who slowly got it done
Don't come for me

Broken means it's changed
Means things have been rearranged
Means that even if it is strange now
It's mine, no matter how
I fought and cried and tried and relied
On every lesson I knew
On and hanging on by a few threads
Don't come for me

Because I can hear the ghosts and I think I see the demons
I think that they'll find me again even
though I was lost for a bit and what I was before,
What I was during
And who I am this moment
Is mine to find
To celebrate
To love and to hate

Don't come for me

Over

I see you standing at the edge of a bridge that's swaying back and forth
Boards rotted and crumbling
Ropes tattered and torn
I wonder how you'll walk across

I've been patching up spots for so long my knuckles have started bleeding
The callouses on my hands are friends I don't really get along with but never leave

You've been a silent spectator for so long, eyes watching, hands in your pocket
You've been on the sidelines walking back and forth, pacing a groove into the dirt

I'm laying down my tools now
I'm taking time for myself
I'm remembering when I missed you
I'm feeling a way that I don't want to

Fix yourself
So maybe we can fix us
But I'm still wondering how you'll walk across

Because I’m still here
I just decided to go quiet
I just decided to rest
I just decided to exhale

Maybe…

There is something very broken here
Shattered pieces everywhere
And some have fallen into holes too deep for me to reach
If I try to put it back together it will be a puzzle with missing parts
An incomplete picture of what used to be

I try to remember a time when we were happy
When we were clean
When we were good

I think it was just a false reality
Because you were never true, you were never real
You wrote stories that you wanted me to read, leaving out parts you didn't want me to know
You still find ways to walk around
Change the narrative
Keep me out
And you think it's just a little bump

But these little bumps have become giant mountains spread out to the ends of the earth
I don't think I have the right gear to climb

I keep casting my truth on hopes but my net is woven too loose
Nothing can stay

You live in chaos, always moving, always looking, never still, noises and bright lights
But I need the stillness of my soul and quiet of my heart to fight through my days
I don't know if there is an in-between.

Maybe...
just let me fall into my own world, allow my peace to spread its warmth
Maybe...
I need a space to call my own where I can find out how to live,
How to be,
Maybe...
I need to close my eyes and go far away from here
Because here has become a place I don't recognize, a place that breaks me over and over

And wake me up when we are healed...

I don't know if I can wake up anymore

Gone

You look past me at the scars that cover my body
At the marks that are left
You decided a long time ago, that's who I am now
Never realizing that those are stains that I can't remove
I can only learn how not to make them again
So you brush past me me like you know who I am now
Never seeing that this story that is so vital to my heart is one that spans years,
Decades,
    Hurt,
      Joy,
        A story that shapes my landscape
Because you think life is a game that you need to win
When no one ever wins
We only pass the time becoming, becoming, transforming, evolving, breaking, creating,
Starting over
And over
And over

And you are missing everything we were going to be
Everything we were going to have
Because those scars, those marks, those beautiful lines of my story hang heavy on your neck,
Too heavy to let go
And find me now, who I am right now
Days go by, nights come too soon
When the darkness remains,
I will be gone

Love

I've come to understand
That I love you
Fully and completely
Deep
In my innermost core
I love you
But you aren't perfect
And I'm not perfect
We're so god damned far from perfect
It's laughable
But we're united in our imperfection
In our dysfunction
You're a little crazy
I'm a little insane
We say stupid shit
We regret words and actions
We find ourselves in pain
But we seem to find a way
Out together
And I watch you sleep at night
Tenderness I've never known
I'm flooded
With truth
Real life
Real beauty

The beauty is in the struggle
The fight to get past,
The past
To live the present
To not fear the future
With you
And it's only the love
Fully and completely
That can breath that life
You are my crazy
I am your insane

Insecure

I know your arms are around me
And in the still of darkness, I cannot see
But you're here
So why isn't my mind clear
Racing, pacing
Wasting time
Walking a fine line
Of love and dread
Of things I should have said
Of things you always say
Of what may stay
Or leave

What if a girl, younger, cuter
Decided you suit her
Likes your smile
And your silly style
The way you smell
And the jokes you tell
The way you play guitar
Just the way you are
The laugh that I love
all of the above

My brain won't rest

Instead I let it fester
That I'm not enough
I'm too rough
Unpolished, tough
Too crazy
It's hazy
Still racing
Still pacing

This is not me, no
Momentary lapse, so
I accept this insecurity
I hope for brevity
Get passed the insanity
Recognize the stupidity
Is based on vanity

And remember your arms are around ME

You

You are strength
There are trials, there are days when the dark
outweighs the light
And moments where you will find yourself lost,
nowhere to go
Remember, you are strength

You are light
There are doubts, doubts that will keep talking
And those doubts will keep coming closer,
wanting to wrap around you
Remember, you are light.

You are beauty
There will be people, who only want to stop you
where you are
Who stand in front, who put up barriers that
seem so high
Remember, that you are beauty

www.ingramcontent.com/pod-product-compliance
Lightning Source LLC
Chambersburg PA
CBHW051750130826
49812CB00033B/1088
9789357210324